Decoding Treachery

WITH SHIELD ANALYSIS

Dale L. Tunnell, Ph.D.

So Bill –
Hope you enjoy !
Dale Tunnell

DECODING TREACHERY

ISBN: 978-1-7334212-3-2

Dedication

I dedicate this book to all those who have been victimized by lies and deceit. The list is long and distinguished.

Acknowledgments

So many people have dramatically influenced my career and contributed significantly to my writing that I struggle to think of the strategies I use in my research that have not been taught or shared in some part by others.

I aim to give credit to those people who deserve special consideration, and thanks for their part in my journey.

Most notably, I must always thank one person, my wife Deborah, for the daily support she gives me and for the clear reasoning with which she provides consistent criticism. She makes me a better person and a better writer.

I also wish to thank a true friend and a real U.S. Marine, Richard Lombardo, who continually motivated me with his humor and encouragement. No day passes that he isn't remarking that I need to get with the program and quit lagging in my daily responsibilities.

I could never accomplish all I do without the inspiration and motivation you both provide me. Thanks for all your help!

Table of Contents

Preface

My name is Dr. Dale Tunnell. I spent 41 years in law enforcement, mostly as a criminal investigator in federal, state, and local departments throughout the United States.

What I learned throughout my career was that in nearly every walk of life, people lie. We are bombarded with lies from 10 to 250 times a day, and the worst possible feeling is when one learns they have been used and victimized by a lie.

I knew that lying has consequences but observing firsthand the impact of someone attempting to cause you harm by lying to you can be devastating. What's more, institutions you learned to trust from a young age have become untrustworthy and wield power for the sake of their benefit and not yours, if even considered.

I learned that victimization occurs because of deception, and I wanted to do something about it. You see, the pain of being lied to and being used can be devastating. It became my mission in life to not only uncover lies but to help other people unmask lies as well.

So, I spent several years gaining specialized training in linguistics, content analysis, psychology, and voice analysis to reach a level of expertise that I could train others to detect deception. I wanted to teach others that by merely listening to someone or analyzing the content of a document, one could recognize a liar and avoid victimization.

With a doctorate in psychology and years of experience in lie detection, I want to teach you a skill set that over 95% of Americans do not possess. You are the reason I wrote this book, and it is my fervent hope that it will help you avoid victimization.

Introduction

Questions for you

Have you ever read a letter or a news article that you didn't feel right about but couldn't figure out why it was bothering you?

Did you ever hear someone tell a story that didn't seem credible, but you were afraid to say anything for fear of offending them?

Have you ever been in a position where your intuition was telling you something was wrong about someone, but you didn't trust your intuition about their lack of integrity?

Have you ever received a text or email from someone, only to learn later that someone intended to cause you embarrassment or financial harm?

What would it mean to you to know with certainty that someone who pretends to be your best friend is being deceitful behind your back?

Have you ever had a loved one tell you something only to learn later they were distrustful? What if you could discover the truth before being blindsided?

These situations happen all the time, and frequently the victim was unable to detect deceit. Does that include you?

What is a Lie?

People the world over consider an untruth as a "lie." However, that's not always the case. A person may say something untruthful, like, "I'll be there shortly," or "I earn about $3000 a month," when neither statement is entirely correct.

Or how about when the wife or girlfriend asks, "Does this dress make me look fat?" Not a comfortable spot to be in if you are a male, you should answer, "You look great, honey," unless, of course, you are completely insane, and you're looking for trouble. What you may be thinking versus what you say are two different processes, so you avoid hurt feelings and lie.

I'm sure you've heard, "Am I getting too fat?" Your wife says, "There's just more to love!" Yeah, right. Most likely, feelings are being considered in these circumstances, too.

The fact is these statements are not so much untrue as they are inaccurate or exaggerated. Technically they are lies, but to what level are they harmful?

Here's one, "It was a perfect phone call," a reference by President Trump to the phone call between President Zelinski of Ukraine and him. President Trump may have believed the call was perfect, but many others did not, and it became foundational to his impeachment.

However, one might ask the question, "Was it a lie, or was it an inaccurate or exaggerated statement?" There seems to be a subtle distinction between the two, but actually, there is a difference.

Specialists interested in cognitive manipulation and deception (CMD) are more specific in their definition.

They define a lie as something that is not only untrue but said for the purpose of fraud.

The intent is to manipulate your behavior by having you believe something said in a manner to exclude the exposure of the truth.

Different Types of Lies

Let's look at different types of lies:

- Jokes
- White lies
- Defensive lies
- Offensive lies
- Embarrassment lies

Jokes

When a person tells a joke, its primary purpose is to entertain. Its communication is usually in jest and isn't associated with stress or deception, (unless you're a comedian and you are looking for laughs). What is essential is not identifying the joke as a deception but determining an emotional range of the person telling the joke. Any ridiculous comment such as, "I just flew in, and my arms are tired," or "My dog thinks he's human," is likely to fall into the category of a joke.

White Lies

How about when you say something to someone to avoid upsetting or hurting them? The primary intent is not to deceive but to prevent embarrassment or emotional pain as in the two examples above. While this is still a form of deception, the purpose and physical reaction differ in comparison to other types of lies.

Defensive Lies

Often the most common form of deception, a person may deny a truthful allegation to protect oneself or someone close to them. A parent may accuse a child of spilling milk on the floor. The child responds that they weren't the one who dropped the milk when, in fact, they did. The response is a defensive lie to avoid responsibility for the act and thus any recrimination or punishment that comes with it.

Offensive Lies

A person tells an offensive lie to gain an advantage that the truth may prevent. This type is less personal and not used to defend against pending recrimination or perceived harm. A deception type often used in advertisement, business, and politics; the minimal expectation of danger is usually diffused and presents little jeopardy to the originator of the lie.

Embarrassment Lie

A lie presented to avoid the embarrassment of any circumstance. A prime example is a statement, "I don't know that woman," or "I never had sex with that woman," when the facts say otherwise.

How about, "That is not my child, I don't even know the mother," embarrassment lies presented recently by Hunter Biden when DNA evidence proved otherwise.

What is a Lie Detector?

A lie detector is any tool designed to determine one's level of truthfulness. The basic premise is to monitor involuntary body physiology to identify and analyze a person's state of arousal, fear, and stress. By using individual sensors to monitor heart rate, blood pressure, respiration, and electrical conductivity of the skin, an examiner can detect measurable differences under stress.

Stress is a result of what we call cognitive dissonance. When two thought processes are not psychologically consistent with each other as in truth or deception, discomfort is triggered and measurable until the speaker resolves the situation. That's why polygraph and voice analysis work. However, due to the need for an examiner's subjective interpretation of the test result, lie detectors are, as a rule, not accepted as evidence in court. The same is valid with the program SHIELD Analysis which we will discuss later.

The expense associated with acquiring, training, and operating a polygraph machine or voice analysis application is usually prohibitive to the average person.

SHIELD Analysis presents a more reasonable approach because the process entails an evaluation of language style and content. The two functions are trainable and significantly less expensive while offering high levels of success.

The human brain plays a large part in the generation of speech and writing. The entire process of thought and speech co-occurs through mindful interpretation, reflecting feelings of confusion, depression, and pain in speech and writing. That's why language is so important. The words a person uses in communication reflects the mental process occurring at the time of the speech or writing. We study this process in what we call psycholinguistics.

We often receive information from media sources such as cable news, op-eds in newspapers, blogs, tweets, internet reporting, and other communications outlets. Most people base their opinions on sound bites and short quips of information without any validating process. The lack of integrity in reporting leads to a misinformed population and divisiveness in the current political and social climate. So how do we enhance our understanding of the information provided us?

One needs to ask several questions:

- How do I sort out comprehensive information from slanted opinions driven by political operatives and discourse?

- How do we identify the misleading and inaccurate communications derived from speeches and testimony?

The answers come from a two-step process.

Step 1:

Know the source of information presented; these are usually danger signs when you see or hear them –

> Specifically identified source
> Sources close to the source
> Unnamed sources

Identify the connections between sources and information outlets.

- Who's married to whom?

- Where was the source previously employed?

- Where does the funding for the source originate?

- What are the general relationships which might impact a factual representation?

- Ask who benefits from the information.

- Get some history of the presenter and put the information into some context.

- Recognize that most media output benefits some agenda or organization.

Step 2:

When written speech is involved, analyze both the content and context of the language using SHIELD Analysis. We do this by examining transcripts and documents containing the written expression.

- Word linkage

- Subjective meanings of each word used

- Relations among words

- Pronouns

- Commitment of statements

- Sensitivity terms

- Changes in language

- Unnecessary language or information

- Hesitations, distortions, repetitions

- Expressions of emotions

- Self-corrections

- Higher/lower-level vocabulary

- Document velocity and structure

Missing Time

When recorded speech is involved, use voice analysis software to identify cognitive processes that might impact validity.

- Psychological disorders

- Drug use

- Deception

- Intensity

- Conflict

- Latency

Benefits of Using Voice Analysis Software

There are benefits to using Voice Analysis Software.

- The subject need not be present during the analysis.
- Language is non-specific – Analysis focuses on acoustical parameters of the voice linked to cognitive processes, not linguistics.

There are drawbacks to full linguistic and acoustical analysis.

- Both processes can be time-consuming.
- Software is expensive ($7,000 to $10,000 for software and training.

The most effective and efficient process for the layperson is to apply the concepts and elements of SHIELD Analysis.

Why is Deception Detection Important?

One would believe the answer to this question is evident because of the harmful impact lying has on the country at large and the individual precisely. We know that deception and deceit can topple governments and businesses and destroy personal lives as well. Saying one should always be on guard against fraud is an understatement if for no other reason than to avoid looking stupid.

But here's a story you might not be aware of, and it will exemplify how a single lie can contribute to the dismantling of the social fabric.

A few years ago, a rather large polling firm conducted human terrain mapping for a burgeoning country. That's bureaucrat-speak for asking a sampling of a country's population about whether they support their government and calculating the percentages. Many of the same processes are used in the United States, except we refer to them as the U.S. Census and political polling.

In this instance, the government of this developing country asked the polling firm to determine what the citizens of that country thought of their government and, in contrast, what they thought of a rather nasty rebel faction.

The polling firm contacted a sizeable random sample of citizens to interview and asked them how they felt about both entities. Overwhelmingly, the citizens reported that they loved their country and fully supported their government. While some were more aligned with the rebels, the results suggested the government was making positive inroads to the betterment of their country's citizens.

The polling firm tallied their results and presented a four hundred-page report to the government along with a personal summary of their findings. Upon completion of the presentation, the government and the representatives of the polling firm engaged in celebration and went home smiling.

There was one hold-out group of individuals, however, who questioned the results of the polling and wanted validation. They requested the polling firm find some way to validate their findings, and so, the firm decided to comply with the group's wishes.

In nearly all cases, the surveyors obtained recorded responses to polling questions, and this provided valuable information for further assessment. The firm gathered samples of those recordings and delivered them to a contractor who specialized in voice analysis. The contractor spent several months analyzing the records and eventually provided their report to the polling firm stating that the firm misinterpreted the original findings.

While most of the population surveyed said they supported their government, the voice analysis showed an opposing view.

It seems that communities were afraid to say otherwise to the polling firm during the survey because they suspected the firm's close relationship with their government and feared retaliation if they told the truth.

Now the firm was in a precarious position. Do they report the new findings or leave well enough alone? Can you guess what they chose? Of course, they took the easy way out and decided not to report the new findings. Instead, they refuted the findings and blacklisted the contractor. Despite the contradictory results, the firm chose to restate its original findings and hoping for the best, remaining mute about the other report.

Unfortunately, there was a revolution and an overthrow of the duly elected government. Chaos reigned, and rebels slaughtered people by the thousands. The result was the formation of an extremist anti-American dictatorship. We now contend with that country regularly.

Had the polling firm been more forthcoming, the small country might have been more prepared to fend off the revolution. On the other hand, truthfulness may not have prevented the revolution, but it couldn't have hurt. Regardless, it seems obvious the role that deception played.

Now, what follows is a series of cases I worked involving real people who found themselves at the mercy of liars. My reasoning for presenting these accounts early in the book is to impress upon you that deception has a consequence.

The degree to which it is hurtful depends on the intent of the person creating the deception. As you develop your skill in this field, you will find that empathy plays a significant role in how you process what you hear or read.

Dr. Jonathan

My friend Jonathan was a very well-known psychiatrist living an affluent lifestyle in California. He was my mentor and contributed significantly to my learning experiences. Jonathan wrote hundreds of peer-reviewed journal articles as well as over 40 books on psychiatric topics such as post-traumatic stress disorder in veterans, mental content analysis, and case studies of victims of psychological abuse. He was professor emeritus at a well-known university, and they even named a psychiatric clinic and institute in his name.

One day, Jonathan received an email from an individual who identified himself as the Nigerian Minister of Finance. In this email, the man explained that he was looking for someone of prominence in the United States who could represent his country's financial interests. He said his country was concerned about the welfare of their assets and wanted to transfer them to a bank in the U.S. but needed a fiduciary representative who was beyond reproach, and they had selected Jonathan because of his credibility and notoriety.

They wished to transfer two hundred million dollars to a U.S. bank, and they would pay him 10% of that total or twenty million dollars for facilitating the transfer.

Jonathan was skeptical at first, but after exchanging numerous emails with the gentleman, the Nigerian convinced him this was the real deal.

Today, this is a well-known Nigerian scam, and it has worn out its welcome. But back then, it was new and was presented with some sense of credibility. To Jonathan, it was a perfect opportunity to secure his financial future. He didn't need the money, but he figured, "Why look a gift-horse in the mouth!"

They convinced him to open an account and place $200k of his funds in the new account to show his good faith. They then invited him to Lagos, Nigeria, to meet with several high-level government officials, and he went. Of course, it was all a scam, and when he returned, he learned the Nigerians withdrew his money and closed the account. He was so embarrassed he kept his loss and efforts to recover his money to himself.

That would be a sad enough story if it ended there. Jonathan knew I was in law enforcement at the time, and to get his money back, he contacted me and asked for my help.

He sent me all the correspondence he received as well as emails and agreements. I examined everything, and I must admit that on the face of the communications, a layperson would have believed it all to be legitimate. However, some clues were in neon if one recognized them. Jonathan did not.

First, the writer of the communication was someone whose first language was not English. A literal translation of the content rather than the context should have alerted Jonathan immediately that something was off. There were so many grammatical and linguistic errors throughout the documents it was evident that no government official wrote them.

Second, changes in terminology were numerous and were representative of convoluted thought in many of the documents.

Guidelines changed several times, suggesting the process was a work in progress and not an established procedure.

There were many more clues easily detectable with SHIELD Analysis that demonstrated this was a scam. Unfortunately, Jonathan only saw the storyline and not the detail. He was unable to recover his losses. To some degree, Jonathan was lucky, though. He only lost his money, not his life. His trip to Nigeria was fraught with danger.

One would believe that a person with Jonathan's credentials would have been astute enough to avoid this fraud. But greed and a lack of skill in psycholinguistics contributed to his victimology. Having investigated many cases of this type, I can say unequivocally, Jonathan wasn't the first to be deceived, nor will he be the last.

Tragically, Jonathan's story took a turn for the worse. Sometime later, Jonathan's children learned of the loss to their inheritance and sued him for control of his funds stating that he was incapable of managing his affairs. I think Jonathan was still capable, but he had been naïve, and the Nigerians took advantage of him.

Ultimately, after hearing the details of the case, the court ruled in favor of the children, and Jonathan lost control of his finances. He couldn't write a check for more than $1000 without a second signature from one of the children. This unfortunate relationship broke Jonathan's heart, and he died a short time later.

There is a moral here. With all Jonathan's education, intellect, and experience in psychiatry, he failed to recognize some elementary danger signals. The most prominent was that the entire approach was unrealistic, and he should have ignored it. Besides, there were ample clues in the correspondence to suggest fraud. Jonathan was lucky to have returned alive from Nigeria. His greed overcame caution, and he lost only his money instead of his life.

Unfortunately, I was unable to help him. Had he asked before engaging the Nigerians, I believe we would have prevented the entire episode either through some simple training or direct action. He wasn't the only one to fall for this scam, but I knew him well, and I know how affected he was with his feelings of betrayal from both the Nigerians and his children.

William and Melissa

William and Melissa had been married for about seven years and lived in a small suburb in the Midwest. For the most part, they got along well and enjoyed life together.

During the latter part of their marriage, Melissa's intuition caused her to notice things were not right with her husband William, and she noticed oddities about his work history, his past life, and explanations of things that didn't add up to her. She couldn't articulate her feelings, but she knew something was wrong with their relationship.

However, she let her feelings pass day by day, still possessed by a nagging feeling. One day while going through the laundry, she was putting her husband's clothes away when she spotted an envelope buried in the sock drawer. Curious, she opened the envelope and read its contents.

The envelope contained a letter to her from her husband explaining that he was not who she thought he was. He had been living under an assumed name in the United States for some years, and though he loved her, he felt he needed to tell her the truth and then leave. At that point, however, he had not decided to give her the letter. He was waiting for the right moment.

You see, William was a Canadian citizen who illegally entered the United States several years before. He stole an identity and used the social security number assigned to that name to obtain legal documents.

After reading the letter, she felt like she just received a punch in the stomach because, until now, she ignored her intuition. Melissa engaged an attorney and filed for divorce.

Luckily for her, most of the property was in her name, and she avoided several legal hassles. The point is, she might have avoided this disaster altogether had she listened to her intuition.

The clues were there all along, but she chose to ignore them. Because she didn't have the training or skill to articulate her feelings after their conversations, she felt she had no basis for disbelieving William. Had she received even minimal training in SHIELD Analysis, she would have discovered his secrets long before the sock drawer.

Of course, the feeling of being used might still be present, but learning this skill would have placed her in the driver's seat much sooner.

Eventually, her ex-husband returned to Canada for reasons unknown. William left behind debt collectors and law enforcement officials looking for him for several years because Melissa was not the only person he defrauded.

After the divorce, phone calls and nasty letters from people looking for William plagued Melissa for several years. No one knows for sure what happened to him, but at least Melissa dumped him before he could do any more damage. She still harbors feelings of betrayal, but she is also now a strong proponent of SHIELD Analysis.

Charlene

Charlene and her husband had been married for 18 years, and one day her husband informed her he wanted a divorce. He told her he was in love with the secretary of their church, and they were going to run off together and get married after the divorce.

Charlene was 41 years old, overweight, with no children and no source of income. As it turned out, the minister of the church learned of the secretary's affair and terminated her employment for issues involving moral turpitude. The position was vacant for some time, and lacking any other opportunities, Charlene applied for the job. The church council offered her employment, and she accepted. Her life was turning around.

She lost weight and was now dating. She had a source of income and was moving forward with her life at a good pace. One day she received an anonymous letter calling her a "slut" and other malicious names suggesting that a woman of her limited moral character should not be working in a church. She was devastated. She wondered if the writer was her husband or even his new girlfriend trying to get back at her.

She received two more letters of the same type only now they were threatening.

This letter campaign was getting out of hand. She received a total of eleven messages in as many days. Charlene contacted me and asked for help.

She sent me copies of all the letters along with samples of writing from her husband and the girlfriend. With a little effort, we were able to determine through handwriting comparison that the first letter was from her husband; the second was from his girlfriend. There was a degree of anger displayed in the writing of the first two letters as a result of the secretary losing her position with the church. Both the ex-husband and his girlfriend were harassing Charlene for the sake of payback. But the remaining nine letters were from someone else.

Charlene had no idea who the second writer was. After examining the remaining letters and applying elements of SHIELD Analysis, we determined that whoever wrote the additional letters knew a lot of details about her personal life, and they had an axe to grind. The writer appeared to have feminine handwriting, and the language was most likely from a female.

Charlene could think of no one who disliked her to the degree exhibited in these letters. There were indications though that the problem was more about her job than it was about her. Numerous comments reflected a familiarization with church procedures as well as the minister and congregation.

As the church secretary, she had access to the previous applications for her position. So, I asked her to review them and search for possible matches to sensitivity clusters we found in the letters as well as similarities in handwriting.

Charlene called me a few days later and told me she found something. Charlene was shocked that someone else wanted her job and was intent on getting it.

Unfortunately, with the position filled, the vacancy closed without success for the anonymous writer.

Subsequently, it seemed there was an all-out push to cause Charlene to quit her job and create a vacancy where the anonymous writer could reapply.

Charlene sent me a copy of one job application she felt might be suspect, and after analyzing it using psycholinguistics and subjecting it to a cursory handwriting comparison, I knew she had found her antagonist.

So, who was the third anonymous letter writer? It seems the minister's wife had also applied for the position, but the church council was reluctant to employ both the minister and his wife at the same time. This disagreement created significant contention among the board members, the minister, and his wife.

Charlene found written correspondence between the council and the minister's wife, which provided corresponding elements identified by SHIELD Analysis to those contained in the abusive anonymous letters.

When Charlene and I engaged the minister in a conference call, he blew his lid and charged that the accusation was absurd. He changed his mind when Charlene showed him the letters and the job application. He knew instantly; his wife wrote the letters.

The Minister presented the evidence to his wife, and at first, she denied everything. Then she broke down crying, telling him how she wanted to be closer to him during the workday and be there to help him with his career.

The minister reported the incident to the church council, and because it was such a scandal, they voted to terminate the minister's employment, stating that they could not condone his wife's behavior nor the impact it might have on the congregation. The minister must have coveted his position more than he did his wife because they were divorced shortly after.

As for the husband and the girlfriend, Charlene filed a complaint with the police, and both were arrested and severely fined on charges of harassment.

The last I heard, U.S. Postal Inspectors were in the process of charging all three for sending threatening letters through the U.S. Mail.

Charlene was now a believer in SHIELD Analysis and, shortly after that, became one of my students. We still correspond even today. Charlene is living happily ever after and now has her eyes on, guess who...the minister.

Nadine

Nadine was an attractive 68-year-old grandmother living a comfortable life in a small community in Florida. Her husband passed away only a year or so earlier, and she was still feeling the effects of being alone. She owned her home, had plenty of income from the life insurance her husband left her, and she had carry-over benefits from his retirement income and social security.

She was living well and had no issues in her life except being lonely. One day she decided that she needed some advice on how she would bequeath her wealth to her daughter. Her husband worked with an insurance agent named William, who handled their insurance needs for several years, and she decided to contact him. He told her he would be happy to assist her and set an appointment to visit her several days later.

When he arrived, he was courteous and extremely knowledgeable about her financial history as well as what she might need to pass along an inheritance to her daughter. After talking for a rather long time, he suggested she gather her legal documents and current insurance papers and meet him at his office in a couple of days.

Nadine gathered everything she needed and visited him, as suggested. He asked her to leave the documents with him so he could examine them more closely, and he would return them later with his recommendations.

Right about now, you're probably thinking, you smell a rat! But not so fast! William did as he promised and returned her documents along with his recommendations. He came up with some excellent suggestions on how she could avoid a substantial tax burden by using life insurance. She liked what he had to offer and said she would like to think about it for a couple of days. They ended their meeting, and she went home.

A week went by, and William had not heard from her. He decided to call and, upon doing so, was greeted very warmly by Nadine. She asked him if he would like to join her at her home for dinner and thinking of her as a potential client, he agreed to meet her. And besides, he was divorced and about the same age as Nadine. There was a physical attraction between the two, and William decided to get to know her better.

The dinner went well, but William detected her loneliness. He stayed long into the evening, talking to her about her life and her deceased husband. She liked him, and more dinners and long evenings became the norm.

William began sending Nadine letters and emails expressing his admiration for her, and eventually, the correspondence became more personal. She learned earlier that he was not married and appeared to be lonely as well. As time went on, she followed his financial suggestions and was satisfied that her wealth was protected; her daughter's inheritance was assured. Nadine and William got along magnificently and saw each other regularly as their fondness for each other grew.

One day she received a call from her banker and seemingly confused, he asked her why she had taken a mortgage out on her home. The house had been free and clear, and there seemed to be no reason for her to do so.

He also informed her that there had been some significant withdrawals from her savings accounts in her name.

Since the banker had been the executor of her husband's estate, he closely followed her financial situation as a favor to her deceased husband. When he noticed these transactions, he became alarmed and notified her.

Nadine panicked and immediately called William. She asked him if he knew anything about the transactions, and he said he did not. He was anxious that she would even consider him as a suspect after helping her so much and developing such a close relationship.

Nadine immediately reported the loss to the authorities, and an investigation began. Bank camera footage identified an older woman resembling Nadine, making the withdrawal from the bank, but identification was impossible due to the degraded video quality. Interviews with the mortgage loan officer and title company personnel suggested similar results. The signor was an older lady who matched Nadine's description, and conversation with the suspect during the transaction disclosed information only Nadine would know.

Nadine was having a come-apart, and she knew she had lost nearly everything due to identity theft. The authorities interviewed William extensively and learned he had suspicions that Nadine might be somewhat unstable. Nothing about William seemed out of place, and since he had established credibility for so long as an insurance agent, the authorities began to look more closely at Nadine.

Looking at a total loss of her daughter's inheritance, a probable foreclosure on her property, and nothing to live on except for her deceased husband's retirement and social security, she became despondent. She felt her life slipping out of control, and she had nowhere to turn.

It was purely coincidental that I had done some investigative work for a friend of her deceased husband. She called him for help, and he presented her with my card.

I received a call late one evening, and she told me who she was. It sickened me that this poor woman had been so taken advantage of, that when she asked me for help, I couldn't say no.

After she described all the events leading up to the loss, I asked her if she retained any of the correspondence between her and William. Of course, he seemed like an obvious common denominator to me considering the timeframe of him entering her life and her financial loss. Luckily, she had retained everything, and she sent me copies of all his letters and emails.

I contacted a friend of mine at the local sheriff's department, with whom I had once worked, and asked him what he knew about the case. What I learned didn't surprise me. William was not a suspect, and of course, suspicion had turned towards Nadine. The investigators suggested dementia, and though they couldn't prove it yet, they believed Nadine faked her crime. With my friend's help, I was able to obtain a copy of the investigative report, Nadine's statement, and William's statement as well.

I used a combination of methods developed in SHIELD Analysis. I was able to determine in a short time that Nadine was telling the truth. I found nothing in her statement that would suggest linguistic conflicts. In contrast, William's deposition was a one-and-a-half-page disaster, and I found approximately twenty anomalies without too much effort that suggested he was deceptive.

The investigators had not asked him to undergo a polygraph examination because they felt his story had been reasonable. Unfortunately, they were looking at the context or storyline he presented rather than the content and detail.

I wrote a detailed report of my findings and submitted it to the authorities. The door opened for a second look at William.

While nothing I provided the investigators was admissible as evidence in court, my report provided several investigative leads to follow up on, and eventually, they decided to re-interview William.

When the investigators showed up at his office unannounced, William became extremely nervous. They went back over his statement and highlighted the anomalies I noted. The investigators also began looking for bank accounts and transactions and included questions about his income.

Eventually, William succumbed to the pressure and broke down sobbing. It seems that he had undergone a somewhat contentious divorce some years earlier, and his ex-wife was hounding him for payment for her half of the settlement. She threatened to take him back to court, and William knew he would lose his business. She also knew about some of his somewhat questionable business dealings and was holding those over his head too.

Along came Nadine with the answer to his prayers. He could get his ex-wife off his back and walk away with some reasonable cash.

He approached his ex-wife to partner with him to defraud Nadine, and she agreed. She was the woman in the video footage. Together, they stole approximately $400,000 from Nadine. Were it not for a coincidental relationship and a business card, Nadine would have been financially ruined.

Psycholinguistics and SHIELD Analysis, along with some excellent investigative follow-up by the authorities, saved Nadine from poverty.

Still, she was in court for some duration to get her mortgage issue reversed, and she only recovered approximately half of the original loss.

Eventually, she sued William and ended up owning his insurance agency's assets. Meanwhile, William and his ex-wife were invited to a rather lengthy stay at a Florida State penal resort at the behest of the Florida courts.

Had Nadine understood the dynamics of psycholinguistics, she might have avoided William's advances. She wasn't alone, though, because the investigators missed the clues also. What amazed me the most was that the anomalies I identified were relatively amateurish and would have stood out to anyone with only minimal training.

Sabastian

Sabastian was a middle-aged man living in California and working in the real estate industry. After a contentious divorce from his first wife, he remarried. This marriage, unfortunately, fared no better than his first, and Sabastian found himself on the defensive end of some severe allegations of family abuse and fraud.

As it was in the first case, a child was involved, but he at least had visitation rights.

Sabastian searched the internet looking for some help when he stumbled across my website, which, at the time, advertised my services as a trainer and practitioner in psycholinguistic analyses. Sabastian contacted me and asked if I could unmask his wife's hidden personality.

Of course, I agreed to help him if I could, and I requested that he send me emails and voice messages he had accumulated over the past period of discord. I was dismayed at what he had in his possession.

He sent me hundreds of emails, and several megabytes of voice recordings he had from messages left him on his phone answering device.

It took me nearly a month to analyze all the data he sent me.

I worked long into the night hours looking at the different configurations of her language, as well as the contrasting accusations and arguments she leveled at him in her voice messages. The difficulty was in the volume of information. It was overwhelming, but I knew I was up to the task.

I read every email and listened to every recorded conversation he gave me. Looking at the context of all the ex-wife's communications from a layperson's point of view, Sabastian appeared to be a dishonest, abusive individual who was so self-centered, he paid little attention to her or their child.

She accused him of committing fraud in his real estate ventures and physically assaulting her on several occasions.

His dilemma was that she provided this same detail to people who would listen to her, and that included law enforcement, social services, and attorneys. The results were as expected. He was arrested and detained, forced out of business, and eventually ruined as a result of her accusations.

No one bothered to check to see if she had prior incidents of this same accusatory nature. Had they done so, they would have learned that she had previously done the same to her ex-husband when she initiated the same patterns of claims against him. She eventually ruined her ex-husband financially and used sympathetic courts against him to obtain substantial settlements.

Sabastian's wife had one other thing going for her. She had a Ph.D. in psychology, and she understood how to manipulate people with whom she came into contact. She was so convincing in her presentations that no one looked deeper into her claims, but instead accepted them on face value.

That's the difference between context and content. Everyone she deceived listened or read only the storyline. They didn't know how to look deeply into the material and detail.

When I completed my analysis, I authored a comprehensive report containing my findings and provided it to Sabastian. Her language was neither sophisticated nor incapable of being analyzed.

Without getting into the detail of the results, the summary was indeed impressive. I found her to be a narcissistic and abusive personality with so much anger directed toward men in general that I warned Sabastian of the danger he faced.

It was clear to me that she was pathological in her deception and was incapable of empathy. She was highly intelligent but overtly irrational. And the danger she presented to Sabastian was that she would stop at nothing to cause him pain.

I also performed the same analysis on Sabastian's communications to her and determined Sabastian to be a passive individual who frequently found himself the victim of aggressive women. He was naïve.

Sabastian believed people were honest and had little reason to lie to him. I found no deception except to say he attempted to conceal his embarrassment at being accused by both wives of being a fraud and an abuser.

More details didn't come out until after his second divorce. Both his current ex-wife and his former ex-wife conspired against him financially. His first wife engaged in other fraudulent activities, and now the FBI is looking for her.

My final report linked linguistic patterns with feigned displays of anger and outrage to produce a highly accurate psychological portrait of a person who was a serial abuser and pathological liar.

Sabastian ultimately presented the report to the divorce court, and the judge accepted it as unbiased evaluation of Sabastian's wife's personality.

Unfortunately, the document was submitted too late in the proceedings and had little effect on the court's ruling. The judge ultimately ruled against Sabastian and in favor of his wife.

Sabastian lost his wealth, his reputation, and fell victim to further degradation, as well.

Knowing Sabastian was in the United States on a permanent visa, his wife filed a complaint with the Immigration and Naturalization Service (INS), who then initiated deportation proceedings against him.

Because of his wife's claim, the INS viewed him as a risk and incarcerated him for months while he awaited a deportation hearing. He became discouraged and disgusted with the American system of justice and took it upon himself to voluntarily leave the country. Sabastian left the United States, never to return. Not only did he forfeit everything he owned, but he also could never have contact with his children.

He was a middle-aged man who returned to his home country, penniless, reputation, and credibility in ruin and forced to live the remainder of his life without experiencing a parental relationship with his children.

Only through the strength of his character was he able to crawl his way back to some level of prominence in his home country. But the loss of his relationship as a father to his children cannot be replaced.

All these experiences were direct consequences of a factor we call C.M.D. In the next chapter, you're going to discover what that means and how you can defend against it. I'm sure that in all these stories, you detected some level of deception involved on my part. The deception is concealment. I concealed the identities of the characters to protect them and their families from further embarrassment. Sometimes, deception is necessary.

What is CMD?

So, let's get started. First, what is CMD? CMD stands for Cognitive Manipulation and Deception. Cognitive manipulation is nothing more than engaging in some form of debate or two-sided discussion.

The intent is to cause a behavioral change in either participant, but most often, the effort is one-way. In other words, I'm telling you something that will cause you to want to change your behavior, so you'll come over to my side in an argument or debate.

It happens in sales, advertising, household debates, and politics. The media does it each time they present you with information, hoping to create an atmosphere, so you say, "Okay, well, I understand that I'm going to come over to your side. I agree with you." That's the whole idea. Get an agreement.

The problem is when deception comes into play. Typically, cognitive manipulation is an acceptable strategy. Even when two people are debating a controversial issue, they're engaging in cognitive manipulation with each other and with the audience.

However, deception is a different function. When falsification is present, it means that the deceiver is trying to manipulate your behavior with some form of falsity. Either by depriving you of information you might regularly use to conclude (concealment), or by outright lying to you about the subject.

The deceiver states something is fact when it is not, in an attempt to cause your behavioral change (a lie).

Most often, deception occurs with such subtlety that victims miss clues that would warn them against accepting an argument as accurate. Advertisers and politicians are famous for doing this.

In the last several years, though, the news media have become expert purveyors of CMD, and unless the public becomes aware and trained to distinguish between fact and fiction, public opinion becomes easily manipulated.

Defending Against CMD

How do we guard against CMD? Well, we use a program called SHIELD Analysis. I used SHIELD Analysis in my research when I wrote my book about Billy the Kid and those who stole his identity. The book is titled **Resurrecting the Dead**, and it's available on Amazon.

Sorry, I just had to plug the book. I also used SHIELD Analysis extensively with clients who were victims of abuse, fraud, and harassment like those stories I described earlier.

What is SHIELD Analysis?

SHIELD, spelled S-H-I-E-L-D is an acronym, and it stands for:

- Strategy
- Heuristics
- Identification
- Emotional and Mental States
- Linguistics
- Demeanor

Each of these categories is part of the analytical process.

Why is it Necessary?

Everyone has some level of intuition. Call it a "gut feeling," a "sixth sense," or even "extrasensory perception (ESP)." However, though you have intuition, you might not always be able to articulate your feelings about the information presented in speech or writing that makes you feel it is not truthful.

You don't need evidence for court, but for you to accept someone is lying to you, you need proof for yourself. You need to have some method you can rely on for your self-confidence.

Tremendous research efforts over the past several years found that human lie detectors are correct only about 51 percent of the time.

But what does that mean? It means that if you hear a story and you say, "Hmm, I don't know if that's true or not. I don't feel comfortable about it, but I'm not certain," you may as well flip a coin, and if it's heads, it's the truth; if it's tails, it's a lie. You'll be about as accurate as an average human lie detector.

Some individuals are better judges of the truth than others. Secret Service agents are very good at lie detection. They range somewhere around 86 to 87 percent accurate, but that's because they must rely on their abilities to do their jobs.

They've had years and years of training, and they have a unique skill that helps them sort out danger signals when assigned to protection details. But most humans don't have that ability without receiving some deception detection training.

Don't rely on a misguided belief that "I instinctively know when someone is lying to me because I can detect when they're feeding me a line."

The bottom line is you can't always do that. Most likely, you're only accurate slightly better than chance, about 51% of the time.

Sometimes, a lie is blatant. You may use body language, or you may detect something in a person's attitude. Their facial expressions or mannerisms tell you that something is not quite right, but most often, you won't rely on your intuition, and you can't articulate the feeling.

Alternatively, we judge that someone is lying when they are telling the truth. Or there is some level of deception through concealment, but the person isn't engaging in an outright lie.

That's where we all make our mistakes. We become arrogant about our supposed intuitional abilities, and we misjudge the information provided. Sometimes we get it right. But mostly, we get it wrong.

I found a way to articulate certain aspects of language that will give you the answers to whether someone is deceptive with you. It's simple, straight forward, and the more you practice it, the better at detecting deception you become.

What's more, by learning these methods, you'll not only identify the liar, but you'll be able to use their language against them.

Now each of the categories in SHIELD Analysis is unique. They consist of multiple guidelines, and we use these guidelines to defend against CMD.

I'm going to provide you with a general structure and describe what's in each category. You will learn a great deal and be able to determine for yourself if you want to continue further training. Most importantly, you're going to learn how to use the psycholinguistic process in SHIELD Analysis to your advantage.

Now I know you're going to ask, "What the hell is psycholinguistics?" Well, this is the science that links the brain to the language a person uses. Up to twelve to fourteen years of age, a person develops their language style, and it doesn't change much beyond that point. No matter how much education they receive, their linguistic style remains constant, and it is identifiable.

An excellent example of this development is a person who grew up on a western ranch or even the Bronx or Brooklyn, New York. The words they use and the style in which they use them remains consistent throughout their lives. It's the same for everyone.

Because language or "linguistics" is a result of thinking or cognitive processes, we can gather specific language patterns to understand the exact meanings of words people use in their spoken or written communications.

Often, when we decipher the correct meanings, the context of a story changes. And we can climb inside their heads to find out what they mean when they tell us something. We use their language to determine whether a story is true or false and, sometimes more importantly, what they are concealing.

What are the Main Functions of Shield analysis?

First, obtain information. Gather all the relevant communication either in speech or in writing. Then we determine what the falsehood is by learning what the writer or speaker doesn't want you to know.

Next, we look at content rather than context. We examine each word. Understand the meaning of each term and recognize relationships with other words. We scrutinize content, not the storyline. Content is the detail. The idea is to examine the content, not the context.

We don't want to listen to the storyline because the storyline isn't detailed enough and can easily mislead the listener or reader. The meaning of a statement is like a carrier wave of a signal. The carrier wave doesn't tell us much but finding and analyzing the signal provides us with boatloads of information.

Get into the weeds, the details, and search for psycholinguistic clues that will tell us what the speaker or writer is saying. We want to use their language and their definitions to impart what it is they mean.

What Does SHIELD Analysis do?

SHIELD Analysis is a is a pretty fantastic tool that examines linguistic patterns. It is a non-intrusive process. In other words, we don't have to strap up a lie detector to somebody. We don't have to test for the galvanic skin response, respiration, heartbeat, or pulse. We don't have to do any of that.

We identify truth and deception, concealed information, and hidden intent by listening to or reading their language. We also recognize the mental and emotional processes. And with all that, we enhance our monitoring and observation skills.

That's important because the more you use this skill, the more intuitive you become. You're not going to hear the story in context; you're going to examine the content and become a more effective listener.

We divide SHIELD Analysis into two symbiotic processes, the first of which is Linguistic Observation. We search for linguistic patterns, word configurations, content rather than context, and specific lexical meanings in the speaker's mental dictionary.

The second process involves searching for emotional and psychological patterns like anxiety, hostility, depression, health issues, etc.

We also look for the existence of psychiatric traits and disorders.

The second part sounds more complicated than it is. Since you are probably not a clinician, you aren't going to provide a therapeutic service, and as a layperson, recognition of psychological or psychiatric patterns is for your benefit, not the speaker. And once you learn the intent is not to reach a clinical diagnosis, it will become easy for you.

At any rate, evaluating both linguistic and psychological parameters is necessary. SHIELD Analysis does so both statistically and subjectively.

Strategy

It's always essential to develop a plan before beginning any analysis. S.H.I.E.L.D. Analysis provides guidelines to help us through the analytical process by suggesting what to do with the information.

There are many fundamentals to be followed and violating any of them will skew your results. They aren't complicated, but it helps to review them before you begin any analysis.

Begin each effort by scrutinizing the document and getting an assessment of the subject and the subject's language. Apply what you know and search for indicators. Above all, analyze the content, word for word, and not the context. Identify the meaning of each word rather than the overall story, as presented.

It's important to note that the body experiences adverse physiological reactions when the subject tells a lie. Sudden onset of anxiety, depressive states, jitters, blinking, twitching, etc. often occurs, and these states provide visual clues that deception may be present.

This physiological response is the reason why polygraph, voice analysis, and body language are useful.

With this understanding, begin your process, giving the benefit of the doubt to the subject and accept the statement as "true."

Subsequently, you prevent an immediate introduction of a "bias" against the person's account, but you will also be alerted when you detect a response, which may be contrary to the reasoning of a truthful person.

Interjecting Personal Belief

Do not add your belief system when conducting an analysis and try to interpret what you think they meant. You will arrive at incorrect conclusions because everything must be assessed based on the subject's understanding, not yours.

Introducing your belief system to a subject's statement will place you on a contextual level and distract from the actual content.

The subject is their editor, and they will tell you what they alone consider essential. It's a matter of choice. They have sole control over what they tell you. If they present you with information, there must have been some reason.

It's up to you to find that reason and decipher the speaker's meaning. You will most likely, formulate an incorrect opinion if you interpret their statement using your interpretation before examining the account from their point of view.

Missing Information

If information is absent, do not insert it to make things fit. If the subject doesn't say it, it didn't happen. If the speaker or writer says something did happen, accept it as truthful but ask, "Could something be missing?"

Grading a Statement

On another note, you are not an English teacher, and you are not grading a paper. Critiquing a statement is a distraction from the primary goal of obtaining information. There may be a legitimate reason for considering the intellect of the subject who provided the story.

Let the flow of analysis guide you to that consideration. Do not reject the account just because the author displayed limited communication skills or inferior intellect.

Firm Commitment

In an open-ended statement, only first person, past tense descriptions are acceptable. Remember that all legitimate recollections are of past episodes. If one remembers a previous incident, the first-person, past tense is the only logical way to present it.

Any other format such as present tense or future tense demonstrates a lack of commitment on the author's part.

Therefore, there is a difference between, "I went home," vs. "I would go home." There is a firm-level of commitment from the first remark, but in the second remark, commitment is lacking.

Look for the commitment in all action statements. A lack of engagement means the speaker or writer is not committed to action, so why should we accept their account as accurate?

Lists

Humans make lists. When speaking of a series of things, places, objects, or people, it is reasonable for a speaker or writer to list in chronological or alphabetical order.

But when the order of appearance is not in either chronological or alphabetical order, the order of appearance often reflects the order of importance to the speaker or writer regardless of whether they are listing names, places, things, incidents, or efforts.

Example:

1. **I took my wife, my three kids, and the dogs to the drive-in.**

2. **After I heard the shots, I looked out the window to see if anyone was in the yard. Then I dialed 9-1-1 and called the police and went immediately to the bedroom to check on my children.**

Statement Legitimacy

Legitimate statements reflect reality. If the account doesn't seem real, it probably isn't. Remember the adage that, "...if the deal sounds too good to be true, it probably is." Well, the same concept is at play here. Sometimes it's difficult to determine if a story is realistic, but when it is not, don't accept it without some further investigation.

We've all heard people remark, "...you just can't make up a story like that." Well, people do make up stories like that, all the time. So, don't just accept it because it is so outrageous. Reality is a great equalizer if you learn to take it as a warning.

Accused of Lying

Never accuse the person providing the statement of "lying." Use some other terminology such as, "You aren't honest with me," or something similar.

Accusing someone of "lying" will undoubtedly cause them to do just that.

An accusation of lying has a psychological impact on people and forces them to barricade themselves with even more falsehoods to reinforce their position of fabricated innocence.

Calling someone a liar is like hitting a fly with a sledgehammer instead of a flyswatter. In this case, the honey approach is better than vinegar.

Mental Disturbance

A mental disturbance does not automatically disqualify information. The mind is an intricate mechanism and relatively easy to unbalance. That said, an incident might precipitate a mental or emotional disturbance but doesn't necessarily make a statement untruthful.

Memory

Constructive memory means the subject read it, saw it on some media, heard it from another person, or dreamed it. For purposes of accuracy, a constructive memory means that the person relating the story did not participate in it. The story may very well be accurate, but the person who is rendering it was not an active player and is relating it second hand. Second-hand accounts are critically important when dealing with eye-witness accounts.

We must always determine the origin of a statement concerning how it was related:

- Did the report originate in a memory?
- Did the statement originate in the subject's memory?

- If from the subject's memory, was it based on the first-hand experience?

We consider the third element, a result of cognitive memory. Only a statement based on cognitive memory, originating in the subject's mind and based on the first-hand experience, can be considered credible.

Heuristics

It is not always possible to apply scientific standards to solve problems. Quite often, we use practical methods not guaranteed to be optimal, perfect, or rational.

Subsequently, we use heuristic methods to speed up the process of finding a satisfactory solution. Heuristics are used frequently in S.H.I.E.L.D. Analysis.

Every person uses unique linguistic and psychological codes in speech and writing. We call this process "psycholinguistics." Identifying psycholinguistic systems provides more information and leads to more accurate conclusions of reliability regarding mental and emotional states.

Truthful statements are realistic because they deal with the past and not the future, and they reflect only personal experience.

Fabricated statements may appear to be realistic, but when they originate outside of the personal experience such as in newspapers, twitter, Facebook, television, or even dreams, they are neither practical nor authentic.

Sensitivity Clusters

A sensitivity cluster is a subjective grouping of cues that highlight violations of S.H.I.E.L.D. Analysis rules. Finding a sensitivity cluster might not indicate deception, but it does justify further investigation.

When you see several clusters, the greater the number, the higher the probability of unreliable information. All sensitivity clusters warrant further investigation.

Linguistic Traits

Linguistic traits developed during the formative years from birth to adulthood cause uniqueness in language processing.

Words may share common meanings among individuals, but linguistic and psychological styles are always different and identifiable. Two people engaged in conversation may be talking about the same thing, but their linguistic patterns may be misinterpreted by each other.

So, back to interpretation. Your interpretation of a person's remarks may not be what they intended for you to understand. Look for changes in linguistic patterns occurring within categories or across categories. That includes stating a point one way and changing it later but still having the same meaning. The changes are what are relevant and, while they may not necessarily be determinants of deception, they should be considered sensitivity clusters.

Configuration of a Legitimate Statement

The average written statement is one to one and a half pages in length. The average verbal conversation is between ten and twenty minutes.

We use the configuration of an account to give us a bird's eye view of whether the statement is generally deceptive. It's not 100% accurate, but it presents you with a quick check.

We divide a statement structure into three parts, and while you probably haven't practiced separating stories into parts since grammar school, it isn't hard to do. With a little practice, you'll spot these separations instantly.

The first issue (1st Trivial Issue - TI) is the introduction to the story. It's usually short but designed to give you some idea of what to expect.

The main issue (Main Issue) is the meat of the topic. It's where the story unfolds, and it usually contains all the detail.

The second issue (2nd Trivial Issue - TI) is the closing or the conclusion. It's also usually short and generally doesn't do much other than to finish the main issue with some form of affirmation.

Count the lines in each of the three categories and round to the nearest whole line. Most true stories consist of a TI-MI-TI duration pattern of 20%-50%-30%.

If you have a long TI then short MI, most likely the statement is deceptive;

If the MI and then TI are the same percentage this is rare but also still misleading;

If you analyze an account where there is only the MI, with no introductory or closing TI, it is also rare but most likely false;

And finally, if the speaker or writer fails to discuss the MI in the first 1/3 of the statement, then deception is probably present.

As earlier stated, this is a quick check you can perform without getting into a detailed analysis.

It helps you focus on what is essential and often keeps you from spinning your wheels. I use this method frequently when I want to prioritize several documents.

Identification

General observation:

If you find one to three sensitivity clusters in a conversation or document, this is a cause for further scrutiny.

Three or more sensitivity clusters suggests a higher probability of deception.

Search for Obvious Constructs

Identify the true definition of each word or phrase. Ask the question, "Does the statement reflect reality?" If not, then this is a sensitivity cluster.

Omissions or Admissions

Is there an admission, or are there omissions? If so, sensitivity clusters exist. Look for a blatant lie and be aware of any psychosocial causations that may be a reason for a statement or phrase.

If you find a comment where you can identify a cause, this is also a sensitivity cluster.

Speech Latencies

The more times a pronoun is repeated, as in, "I, I, I," the higher the level of anxiety exists. A repeated pronoun generally reflects the emotional state exhibited at the time of the statement. (Sensitivity Cluster)

Example:

I – I – I don't ---- I – I don't know what made me do it. I don't, I don't, I don't, I mean, If I look at it now, it doesn't even feel like I – I did any ---it-it just ----I don't know. I don't – I don't – I don't know. I just don't –I...

You can tell whether written or audible, this person demonstrates extreme anxiety. It would be prudent to look deeper into content and follow up on other sensitivity clusters.

Hesitations and Interjections

Hesitations and interjections of non-words usually indicate anxiety and possible confusion. These non-words include utterances such as "uh, ah, er, uh-huh, uh-huh, etc."

The more utterances used, the higher the level of anxiety. One can quickly identify utterances. Hearing or seeing these utterances indicates a deceptive strain embedded within the story and is a sensitivity cluster.

Crossed Out or Erased Words

When a word has been scratched out or erased and a replacement word used, there may be confusion, but this is a sensitivity cluster, and you should scrutinize it.

Multiple changes suggest deception. The most crucial factor is the original word that was scratched out or replaced. Look closely at how this replacement changes the meaning of the statement.

Example:

After the fight and John was lying on the ground, I ~~walked~~ ran to the telephone to call the ambulance. Uh, I mean I felt him first to see if he was still alive, and then I went into the house to find a telephone. He was bleeding pretty bad and I ... there was blood on the ground coming from the ~~wou~~ ...injury and I tried to help him as best I could.

The crossed-out words have a significant impact on the statement and paint a different picture than the corrected version.

Higher/Lower Level Vocabulary

When a person uses higher-level vocabulary than when the conversation calls for, you should suspect deception.

An example would include vocabulary, which would not be generally expected during a statement unless the speaker was highly educated and known to use such terms.

In other instances, quite the opposite might be present. Lower-level vocabulary might exist to appear more common. Examples might include street language or slang when the circumstances are not warranted.

Any use of either higher or lower vocabulary when it does not happen naturally is the result of deception and should always be viewed as suspect and referred to as a sensitivity cluster.

Example:

1. **(Bank executive's statement.) After the bank was robbed, I knew you guys would point the finger at me and try to lock me up. I don't deserve to be collared for something I didn't do.**

2. **(Bartender's statement.) I would expect the perpetrator would be incarcerated within a short period. However, the ramifications of one of us being a suspect never occurred to me.**

These examples are overly simplified, but you get the idea.

Linguistic Velocity

We measure the velocity and configuration of a statement by the amount of unimportant and mundane information used to tell a story. We measure speed against what we refer to as "objective times."

"Objective times" are times within the statement that we can point to with specificity, such as, "I went to the doctor at 1:00."

We can look at the clock and say that this person accomplished a task at an exact time. Alternatively, we cannot know whether a person attended their appointment in the statement if they said, "I had an appointment for 1:00."

This time we describe as "subjective time." There is a finite difference between the two statements, although they are very close.

We distinguish between specified times in this manner:

➢ Objective Times (OT) - Those times when something happened.

> Subjective Times (ST) - Those times when something is projected to happen but cannot be confirmed.

Example:

My delivery was expected by 2:00 p.m., but it actually showed up at my door at 6:00 p.m. that evening. While I waited for the package, I had a few whiskeys and fell asleep around 3:30 p.m. I awoke when the delivery man rang my doorbell. It was straight-up 6:00 o'clock. I don't know where all the blood came from.

The first time, "2:00 pm" is a subjective time since the delivery was only expected but not confirmed. The second time, "6:00 p.m." is the objective time since we know the delivery took place. Also, 3:30 p.m. and 6:00 o'clock are also objective times. Note there is missing detail for the period between the two objective times. Whatever happened, it probably occurred between these two times.

Here's an example for you to wrap your mind around. In a statement where there are two lines between two times given to be 10 minutes apart, we calculate 12 lines per hour (60 minutes = 1 hour, 60/10=6, x 2 lines = 12 lines per hour). This calculation might be a baseline for future changes in velocity.

Just go back to basic math. (I know you never thought you would have to use it after high school, but here it is again.) We focus on missing information or changes. Changes in velocity within a statement identify significant events and is a quick way to locate unaccounted for gaps in time and omissions. Not all accounts have objective times.

Changes in velocity may also indicate a sensitivity cluster due to the speeding up or slowing down of the statement in a peculiar location. It's that change we're looking for because the shift provides us with a clue that something significant happened between the two differentials.

Example:

I met my girlfriend for breakfast at 10:00 at McDonald's. We talked about our families, what they thought about us dating, and what she wanted out of our relationship.

Our conversation lasted about ten minutes because I was already bored because we had the same conversation yesterday. I'd had enough and I got up from the table and left the joint at 10:10 am.

I headed back to my apartment, expecting that she would call me and try to smooth things over, but I stopped off at my friend's house around 11:10 and stayed there until I was ready to go home. I finally got home around 6:00 p.m. and while I was watching the news, I heard them say my girlfriend was murdered.

Using the objective times in this statement to compute velocity, we note that between 10:00 and 10:10, the line velocity was approximately 24 lines per hour (60 min. divided by 10 minutes =6; 6 x 4 lines between the two times equals 24 lines per hour).

The line velocity between 10:10 and 11:10 is two lines per hour (60 min. divided by 60- or 1-hour difference between the two times equals 1; 1 x 2 lines equals two lines per hour).

Since we don't know for sure what time he departed his friend's house, we can't consider the third objective time of 6:00 p.m.

On the other hand, the significant reduction in line velocity from 24 lines per hour to 2 lines per hour was dramatic and suggests that he is concealing information, a sensitivity cluster. He most likely killed his girlfriend during this time.

Time Disparity

When we identify objective times, but there is no description or definition of events between them, there is a time disparity. In other words, some gaps cannot account for past tense activity.

Missing information between two objective times may indicate unintentional omission but could also mean the intentional omission of crucial information. Generally, this disparity is the moment of the commission of a crime or incident and should be considered a sensitivity cluster.

Example:

We had a full crowd that night, and it was hard to keep track of all the money coming in. The boss has always told me to close before 2:00, so after putting the money in the safe I closed the bar down at 1:45 a.m. At 2:00 a.m. I was on my way out the back door when someone hit me from behind. I don't know how long I laid in the doorway. One of the local cops spotted me I guess when he made his rounds. The next thing I remember, it was around 2:30 when the medics were bandaging my head.

The theft took place between 1:45 a.m. and 2:00 a.m. The employee took the money and staged a robbery. See if you can solve the crime with what you have learned. Hint: Use language velocity for your answer and look for missing information.

Minutia and Trivial Details

When unnecessary information or language in the topic of discussion occurs, there might be an instance where the listener or reader might ask, "Why would they tell me that?" Or there might be so much detailed minutia that the story becomes a rambling mess.

There may be two considerations. The first is that, although the listener or reader does not consider the information relevant, the writer or speaker is the one editing their own story and can include whatever they choose. We discussed that earlier. The speaker or writer considers the information essential and therefore includes it in their account.

In this circumstance, the listener or reader must consider this information extremely important because it must have some relevance, or the writer or speaker would not have included it. The entire process of minutia or trivia must be considered a sensitivity cluster.

Secondly, an unsolicited volume of irrelevant information is usually indicative of a person attempting to evade sensitive issues. They focus on minutia in hopes that the analyst overlooks the real problem. Pay attention when the speaker asks a question of the listener or reader out of order.

As an example, the speaker asks the listener or reader, "Do you want me to stop," while describing a physical assault. The significance of this question is that the speaker might be reliving the experience, and they asked that question of the victim at the time of the incident. Both circumstances are sensitive clusters.

Example:

I knocked several times on the door, and no one answered. So, I tried the door to see if it was unlocked and it was open so I went inside. I yelled for Mrs. Johnson to see if she was OK and there wasn't any answer so I went on in to see if ~~anyone~~ anything was alright.

The light was on and there were little glass beads on the floor. I could hear the wind blowing outside. It sounded like ~~someone was screaming~~ a banshee and there was a chill in the air.

Winters can be so cold up here even without the wind. That's when I saw Mrs. Johnson lying on the floor with the gun beside her and her pants down.

Find the minutia and the crossed-out words to figure out what happened. If you determined that the man killed Mrs. Johnson, you would be correct. Spot the sensitivity clusters and mark them. The story rewrites itself.

Emotional and Mental States

Determine the Emotional and Mental State of the Individual

As a layperson, there is no need for you to use a psychological or psychiatric assessment tool. Disorders might affect the outcome of an analysis, but you are operating at a rudimentary level much lower than that of a therapist or clinician.

There are some tools available, albeit more for the professional than for the layperson. But most are written instruments designed to test the individual for several psychiatric or psychological issues, and one needs extensive training to interpret them.

The problem with using these tools is that the individual must volunteer to take the tests, and giving tests isn't your role. You aren't a clinician. And, unless you are skilled at interpreting these instruments, it's a waste of your time.

I prefer software applications that I can use at my leisure, and I don't need the subject's permission. I prefer a software program called PCAD3. That stands for Psychiatric Content Analysis and Diagnosis 3, which is the 3rd version of the original software application.

The cost is about $300 and available to anyone. The developers did not design the program for a layperson, but it is easy to use. And when coupled with SHIELD Analysis, one gets a comprehensive view of not only the story but the storyteller as well.

There isn't a need to get more into this program at this point. In the advanced training, I cover the use of PCAD3 in detail as it does take some practice. But as I said earlier, you would use this only if you were pursuing this program as a professional.

A more critical function for you, though, is simple observation and an understanding of specific traits one might want to learn about so they can recognize them when observed. Don't let the words scare you. For the most part, you already know how to spot these issues.

These traits consist of:

- Anxiety (stress)
- Hostility (anger)
- Depression (morbid sadness)
- Health (sickness)
- Quality of Life (view of their own life)
- Social alienation-personal disorganization (hearing voices and being scattered)
- Hope (outlook)
- Cognitive Impairment (reduced learning or thinking ability)
- Human Relations (get along with others)
- Achievement Strivings (motivations)
- Dependency Strivings (relying on others)

I reduced all these trait descriptions for simplicity's sake, but the layperson, learns to spot them, and their recognition can add significantly to an assessment.

State of Mind

We all know proving "intent" or "negligence" in a court case is critical in assessing blame for the commission of some anti-social act. The same is true when determining the degree of deception. We want to know if the rendering of information was intentional or was accidental.

Was it one of the types of lies I referred to at the beginning of the book that had some social justification, or was it deliberate deceit? It's one of the factors we examine when scrutinizing language.

Remember this. Statements always demonstrate the state of mind of the person who made them. Always look for firm, active verbs, or passive terms with exaggerated importance.

Both parameters will provide you with an accurate assessment of the person's intent, and you will answer the question of whether the information was an intentionally deceptive offensive or defensive lie or just a social response such as a joke, white lie, or the result of embarrassment.

Medical and Substance-related Issues

When evaluating a statement, one factor that may have a dramatic impact on the accuracy and relevancy is whether the speaker or writer has a medical or a substance abuse issue.

How the person is feeling can often impact the outcome of your evaluation. If they have a medical problem and aren't feeling well, they may not present adequately, causing you to misread details.

If substance abuse is an issue, this could be foundational to intensified feelings of persecution and create the need to be deceptive.

One may have nothing to do with the other. The appearance of deception may result from their intent to conceal their condition rather than to present falsified information. Just be aware that deception appears for many different reasons.

Observation

A layperson predominately exercises personal rather than professional inspection. You, the layperson, are not seeking clinical diagnosis as defined by DSM V (Diagnostic and Statistical Manual for psychiatric disorders).

You are only looking for possible mental states that might clarify your findings. Recognition of the existence of poor mental health adds to or detracts from validity. Complications may not be readily apparent, but different types of mental states may be detectable.

You may confirm or alter the relevance of information. The critical thing to remember, though, is mental disturbance DOES NOT disqualify information.

Demonstrative Emotions

Descriptions of emotional distress generally occur after the crisis has passed. Remember that the storyteller relates the story from memory, and only the storyteller knows the details. If emotion is expressed before or during the crisis while telling the story, deception is probably present, and this is a sensitivity cluster.

The absence of emotion in circumstances where reality would suggest it should be present may be as telling as misplaced emotional responses. Lack of passion is also a sensitivity cluster. An example might include the general demeanor of a family who lost a loved one.

On the surface, they may appear uncaring or non-committal. What is happening underneath may be quite different. Military and first responder families often display stoic reactions until they are in a private environment where the public cannot observe them breaking down in despair. Do not draw an automatic conclusion without some further investigation.

Example:

1. **I was walking past the dumpster when the man came out from behind it. I was extremely afraid. Then he pointed a knife at me and told me to give him my wallet.**

2. **I drove down the dark street grimacing with fear because I didn't know what might happen when all of a sudden, the man stepped in front of my car and pointed a gun at me. He came to my window and told me to get out. I got out of the car, and he forced me to go into the bushes. While he was holding the gun on me we had sex. I was so scared while he was whispering what he was going to do to me. I finally passed out from fear and I don't remember what happened after that.**

Here are a few clues to both examples. In example #1, it is apparent a man coming from behind a dumpster while you are walking past might elicit some level of fear. If you were a previous victim before, the fear might even be extreme.

Example #2 appears to be a falsification. The person was "grimacing with fear" before anything happened. What's more, as an analyst, we're not interested in what might happen, only what did happen.

Additionally, the person making the statement could not possibly have known what might happen, and to make this remark in an open-ended account is highly suspicious.

"All of a sudden," is another clue that deception may be present because this is an unwarranted interjection, and as you will learn in more advanced training, these types of interjections nearly always indicate deception.

The remainder of this statement is deceptive because of the passive verbs used in the description of the sexual act, "we had sex" instead of "he raped me." The sensitive clusters suggest this was a consensual act told to conceal information from someone, possibly a husband or boyfriend.

Linguistics

Pronouns

Specifically, we want to examine the use of "I, we, they, you, us, them, mine, yours, theirs, etc.," to identify issues like the number of persons present, their closeness, possession, distance, affection and many other examples. If an analyst can master the concepts of pronoun evaluation, even without further analysis, the quality of an inquiry can be enhanced by as much as 50%.

Example:

We were walking along the sidewalk when a man jumped out from behind the bushes and grabbed me. We wrestled for a few seconds and he threw me to the ground, then he turned on Sara and Jean. Sara screamed and kicked the man while Jean hit him with her pack. A bottle fell out of her pack, and she smashed it on his head. We were able to fight him off until he ran from us leaving a trail of blood.

By referring to the pronouns in this story, fourteen in all, one can get a clear picture of how many people were involved and who the victims were.

Changes in Verb Tenses

The rule when making a statement about something which occurred in the past is to use the past tense. When a change in tense is apparent during the account, you can deduce that there is a degree of sensitivity, although not necessarily deception. Consider this a sensitivity cluster but look deeper for causation.

Example:

I was drinking in the bar when the fight started. The big bruiser picked up the bottle of beer and poured it on my head. He would taunt me and call me names and then say, "You little pervert, I ought to kick your ass." He tells me that he wants to beat me up, and then he tortures me by pushing my head down on the table and he whispers in my ear that he hates homosexuals. I fought him as hard as I could but I wasn't strong enough to stop him. He hits me two or three times and I passed out on the floor.

Pay close attention to the changes in verb tenses and remember the rule of commitment. If you discerned that the alleged victim started the altercation, you would be correct. The embellishment was an attempt to make the situation look like a hate crime. The victim passing out on the floor was not a result of an assault but rather a simple case of too much liquor.

"Say, said," vs. "Tell, Told."

"Say" and, "said" during a conversation generally indicates a passive, non-aggressive setting during the discourse. "Tell" and, "told," on the other hand, suggests a more aggressive and animated situation.

The use of either set of these terms may enlighten the analyst as to the emotional environment in which the discourse is occurring.

However, a change in usage from "say" or "said" to "tell" or "told" is extremely important and might signify an escalation of emotion such as anger or frustration. You should consider this change as a sensitivity cluster.

"This" vs. "That"

When used as a descriptor, these two terms indicate proximity to the speaker. They may be referring to an object or a circumstance. Pay close attention to their usage when there is an unexpected change. A change indicates distancing from the particular purpose or condition and is an indicator that something, in reality, changed to cause this transition. Never neglect this change and consider it as a sensitivity cluster.

Linguistic Array

A linguistic array includes phrases and words used in one part of the statement compared to a changed usage in other locations but still having the same meaning. An example of a linguistic array is, "I knew the game was up," used in variation several times during a statement and then suddenly appearing as "I knew they found us."

The phrases mean the same, but the change in usage suggests that something has happened within the statement to cause this change. **NOTHING IN A STATEMENT HAPPENS IN A VACUUM!** There is a reason for this change and should be considered a sensitivity cluster.

Linguistic Variance

Changes of language can demonstrate how a person feels about someone or something and can often pinpoint the moment in which those feelings change. It is also a mechanism to identify radical changes in the statement.

An example would include several comments during a conversation referencing "the kids" or "my kids."

A transition to "the children," especially after "my kids" got into trouble, suggests the parent was not a happy camper. Seeing these changes are usually prominent and should be considered as sensitivity clusters.

Example:

My girls have always been a bit boisterous but never outrageous. When I was told that they broke into the house, I was shocked and disappointed. I picked the girls up from the police station and took them home. After I read the police report and heard their side of the story, I sent the children to bed without supper.

Notice the change from "my girls" to "the girls" and then ending up as "the children." A fall from grace and in such a short time.

Here's another **example** you can try for yourself.

I was riding my bike along route 60, traveling at about 50 when I noticed this hot roadster with a gorgeous blonde driving it. She was about 100 yards ahead of me so I slipped up beside her and waived. The blonde acted like she never noticed me so I beeped my horn at her.

The blonde turned and looked at me and then whipped the car over into my lane. I had to kick the side of the car to keep my balance and I suppose I left a dent in the side of the door.

The blonde was really pissed and began yelling at me. I looked closer at the blonde and was surprised to see his mustache blowing in the wind. I really didn't do anything on purpose to his car. I was just trying to protect myself.

Who was responsible for this incident? Was the rider of the motorcycle truthful in his testimony? The answer was, "NO!" See if you can figure it out. There are three simple clues pointing to deception. See if you can find them.

Linguistic Observation

When examining communications or stories, there is a pattern to be followed by the examiner. By moving methodically down the list, you are less apt to overlook a process that might net you some valuable information.

Once you follow this process a few times, it will become automatic, and you won't have to think about it or refer to some cheat sheet. Together these individual parts create a mosaic that formulates a comprehensive picture.

Begin your efforts with written documents so you can refer as necessary. Eventually, your listening skills will perform these processes too, and little, if anything, will get by you.

- Look at the statement as a blueprint
- Examine the Foundation
- Examine the Structure
- Examine Individual Parts
- Usage

- Placement
- Frequency
- Verb Tense
- Grammatical structure
- Phraseology
- Specific meanings of words
- Different interpersonal relationships within the statement
- Crucial locations of words and phrases
- Changes in usage between words and phrases

Commitment

We talked about this earlier, but I want to reinforce how vital commitment is. Without commitment, one cannot realistically assess the intensity of a person's statement. And it's the intensity that provides you with a clearer picture of credibility or deception.

Of course, people can mask their true intentions, but if you remain alert, a deceptive person will eventually trip themselves up and give you the evidence you need to determine their validity. It may take more than one episode. If your intuition is telling you that the person is not truthful, stay with it. You may not discover the truth, but you will see the lie.

Just remember that a statement must demonstrate commitment. Hearing or seeing the pronoun "I" in a first-person, past-tense description demonstrates commitment and connection to the past. "Did not" is stronger than "Would not." Noncommittal examples include: "might," "maybe," "probably," "possibly," etc. and conditional future tense such as "would," "could," "should," etc. are sensitivity clusters.

Example:

I already told you, I did not take that diamond from the display case. I would never steal diamonds from Mr. Takiuchi. He's a wonderful man. It might be that someone who was in the store after I got off work probably stole the jewelry. On second thought, I might have mislaid the diamond somewhere else in the store.

Look for the non-committal word in her statement and notice the changes in tenses. Note that she did not take the diamond from the display case. She demonstrated strong commitment here. She stole the diamond from another location in the store as she admitted to "mislaying it."

Counting the sensitivity clusters in a document or conversation provides you with an overview of the truthfulness of its contents. Of course, the more you find, the clearer the picture becomes. The importance of sensitivity clusters is that they provide you with areas for further investigation. Clustering doesn't necessarily mean someone is lying but the person may be involved in deception by concealment or omission.

Finding thirty to fifty sensitivity clusters in a statement is not uncommon for someone intent on deception. Deception has a "pile-on" effect. The more a person lies, the more they must add to the lie. Otherwise, the foundation of their story crumbles and the listener discovers the fabrication.

Demeanor

Assessing demeanor is crucial to a successful evaluation in SHIELD Analysis. The more you know about both types, the more effective you will be as an analyst. Conduct these two evaluations after you have performed your assessment of the discourse, communication, or story. These evaluations will help you determine the relevancy of your analysis and increase your confidence in your abilities.

Subject Demeanor

If possible, it helps to get an assessment of the contributor. If engaged in a conversation, simple observation is often adequate. However, this is not so easy when evaluating writing from an individual. There may be some record of the individual, or you may know someone who has firsthand knowledge of the person's personality.

Knowing something about the target of your assessment arms you with more details and allows you to determine the credibility you might assign to them.

 Look for these traits:

- Orderly-obstinate – intellectual
- Optimistic – impulsive
- Greedy-demanding – requires gratification

- Anxious and Self-centered – intensely vain
- Guild-ridden – faults others for past wrongs
- Wrecked by success – failure in life
- Schizoid or strange – experiences a fantasy world
- The Exception – the world owes him or her
- Average or typical – no dominant characteristics

Analyst Demeanor

Take stock of yourself and perform some self-reflection both about your level of proficiency and your reasoning ability. If you do this each time you engage SHIELD Analysis, you will find that character judgment will improve dramatically.

You won't have to wait for the formal analysis to draw your conclusions. Instead, you will notice a distinctive improvement in your ability to size people up and protect yourself and others against CMD. And, it will enhance your success as an analyst.

Ask yourself these questions:

- Are you empathetic?
- Are you curious?
- Have you put substantial effort into your training?
- Are you a detailed person?
- Are you persistent?
- Above all, can you control your bias?

These are all factors contributing to your success. If you lack any of these factors, their absence is not catastrophic. You will still amaze yourself at what you learn when engaging SHIELD Analysis.

Exercises

I've added some practice exercises for you so you can work on what you've learned. These are actual cases of statements taken during interviews at some point in an investigation. Some are more difficult than others but have fun with them. There was a real outcome in each case.

The exercises all have several clues to help you locate sensitivity clusters and determine for yourself whether there was deception present.

Pay attention to the statement configuration at the bottom of each statement and follow the rules. Because of the print configuration of the book, the numbers may be off a bit. So, if you do a real count, they may not match exactly.

In those instances, use the numbers I provided. Then go back and dig deeper. In each case, I left the final decision up to you. You will find the answer to which exercises were deceptive at the end of this chapter. Have some fun and see what you have learned.

Exercise #1 (Teddy Kennedy-Chappaquiddick)

I was driving my car on Main Street on my way to get the ferry back to Edgartown. I was unfamiliar with the road and turned right onto Dike Road, instead of bearing hard left on Main Street. After proceeding for approximately one-half mile on Dike Road, I descended a hill and came upon a narrow bridge. The car went off the side of the bridge. There was one passenger with me, one Miss Mary Jo Kopechne.

Configuration: 6 ½ lines = 100%
1st TI = 1 ½ lines = 23%
MI = 4 lines = 61%
2nd TI = 1 line = 15%

Exercise #2 (Homicide)

I have don't why they said that sir, I have no idea who this man is, I have no knowledge of this crime, I was not involved in this crime, it caught me by surprise when mom got a hold of me about this. I didn't think you would tell me where you got that information. I don't know why you was told that. I am willing to take a lie detector test. I am willing to prints, whatever you need. I do not know this man, I am not involved in this. I have no knowledge of this crime.

Configuration: 7.5 lines = 100%
1st TI = 3.25 lines = 43. %
MI = 1.5 lines = 21%
2nd TI = 2.75 = 36%

Exercise #3 (Homicide)

I met him...I have some friends that were looking for a friend and I was told these people were moving back to California and had a bunch of furniture they were trying to sell and they had a really nice aquarium, went over there and she wanted fifteen hundred bucks for it. Got out of rehab in December...moved to Carl with Johnny. The first of February my mother my picked me up to go to Kansas cause my aunt was in the hospital, was there about 2 weeks. I went back to Clyde and about 3-4 days later she died. I went back to Kansas and was there about another 6 or 7 weeks and I had my uncle's car. I guess he got released from jail in Del Rio so I brought his car back and I was gonna get my pickup and get back to Kansas. I was planning leaving here in about three weeks.

Configuration: 12.5 lines = 100%
1st TI = .25 lines = 2%
MI = 4.25 lines = 34%
2nd TI = 8 = 64%

Exercise #4 (Homicide)

I mean, I think it was a-a-a-a bunch of things. / Uhhh, ya know, uh, financial, uhh, financially, ya know, how I fucked up and they would find out and I stole money from 'em. And I hated my job. I hated what they wanted me to do for a living.

I hated-hated being around them. I hated everything. / [They complained] about anything. Weight, uh, work, I'm a slob. I don't do anything around the house. Uh, you know you don't spend time with us, what are you doing.

Stop smoking pot. Ya know, it was always something. I mean you can't even drive the car without her nagging.

Configuration: 9.25 lines = 100%
1st TI = .75 lines = 8%
MI = 4 lines = 43%
2nd TI = 4.5 = 49%

Exercise #5 (Natalie Holloway-Joran Vandersloot)

I didn't make up any of that. I mean, we were there, and they said OK, well, then let's go to the Holiday Inn. And you know, we got in the car with—with the police officers, and they went in the van. And then we went there. I mean, that's the only—just—me and Deepak, we didn't get a chance to talk to each other at all about it to actually make up, you know, a story.

So it was basically making it up as we go along. I mean, and we got out—and we got out, and Deepak said, Oh, yes, there were two security guards there that saw her-that saw her when she got—when she stepped out of the car.

And that's what—that's what he told the police. And I was like, you know—that's what—now, if you also look back at that, you're like—I mean that's –that's horrible. They got arrested and held for ten days because of this. That's really—I mean, that's something that you know, I can't forgive myself for, either.

When I was at the police in Nord, I had this—one of the guys was next to me. And you know, he was always happy. He was always singing and talking about his—about his wife and kid.

And I was in the cell next to him. And I was talking to him too, you know?

He was really, you know, a nice guy and you felt so guilty that it was your fault that, you know, he got arrested. That's something, you know, you feel horrible for.

Configuration: 14.5 lines = 100%
1st TI = .33 lines = 2%
MI = 9.5 lines = 66%
2nd TI = 4.66 lines = 32%

Exercise # 6 (Homicide)

And I, uh-I swung the pipe, um, the coat rack and I hit him two or three times. He went down on the couch, and I don't know what I did with the pipe at that point. I, I looked for the gun. I looked under the couch, looked in his pockets, looked in his jacket and looked everywhere.

Looked in all the couch cushions, under the couch, under the chairs. I-when I was looking I lifted him up and I put, I layed him on the couch like he was laying down.

Again I was looking, I went, looked in his pockets, found money, put it back, went looking for the gun and two or three times, I went in his pocket and I found the money.

And, I put it back and then when I couldn't find the gun I was-I saw what I had done and I was distressed and I grabbed the money and put the jacket over top of him, pulled it over the top of his head...

Configuration: @9 lines = 100%
1st TI = 1.75 lines = 19%
MI = @ 7.25 = 81%
2nd TI = 0 lines = 0%

Exercise #7 (Homicide)

Uhhh, well, the first thing I did is I walked in, went to the bathroom. Walked back out, picked up some luggage, brought it back in the house from the trunk.

And then I walked into my bedroom, grabbed the gun and a pillow, I stepped out—I walked out of the bathroom bedroom into the office, and I shot him from behind. And my mother was in the bathroom, heard it, and said, "What the hell's wrong?" blah, blah, blah. She walked out, and I popped her.

Configuration: 8 lines = 100%
1st TI = 1.25 lines = 16%
MI = 4 lines = 50%
2nd TI = 2.75 lines = 34%

Exercise #9 (Arizona State Prison Escape)

Yeah, he swung it like a baseball bat, struck me across the left side of my face, and I went flying. I didn't get knocked out, Thank God. That was about 6 o'clock. Um, Officer Byron saw what he did and attacked him, the Smith hit him with either his fist or that paddle and took his cuffs, secured him, came after me, and he had to stumble around to find a locked door in order for him to secure me.

At about 6:15, he asked me if I knew how to operate an AR-15, because he saw it laying there right on the table, and um, he looked around for the magazine. I had to show him how shut the slide. I had to show how to turn off the safety and how to turn it on. How to re-set the slide if he had to routinely move around or whatever the case may be.

Then I had to explain all the ammo that was in the ammo locker and um, we kind of briefed him, briefly, on how to use the control panel because all that he was after is getting out.

At 6:30 he stopped asking me questions. At 6:45 I saw the guards running across the compound and I figured they were going to assault the building. Smith started yelling at me and Byron and I figured he was going to shoot us.

Configuration should be: 20%/50%/30%
Actual: 1TI=33% MI=46% 2TI=26%
Linguistic velocity between: 6:00 and 6:15 = 60 min in 1 hour/15min segment=4, x 3 lines = 12 LPH
Linguistic velocity between: 6:16 and 6:30 = 60/15=4, x 6 lines = 24 LPH
Linguistic velocity between: 6:30 and 6:45 = 60/15=4, x 1 line = 4 LPH

Answers

All nine statements were deceptive but for different reasons. Some were deceptive due to concealment of information or simply missing information. Others contained outright lies.

In several instances, there were substantively truthful facts contained within the accounts. Distinguishing between deception and truth in each helps you sort fact from fiction and provide clarity and validation.

The point is you are the arbiter of what matters. You are responsible for assessing weight to the falsehood and it is your determination alone, that classifies a statement as deceptive or truthful. That's why we call this type of analysis, subjective.

One final point. In the last exercise, something extremely sensitive occurred. The second officer was a female and she was sexually assaulted. Can you locate the timeframe when it transpired?

SUMMARY

Probing with SHIELD Analysis

➢ The analysis consists of Crucial Indicators, Patterns, and Multiple Relationships.

➢ Consider both psychological and linguistic relationships.

➢ Misinterpretation may have only a minor impact on the overall analysis. You will make mistakes, but they will be fewer the more you use SHIELD Analysis.

➢ Practice reduces errors.

➢ Visual stimuli enhance performance.

➢ Continued practice stimulates auditory recognition.

➢ "Intuition" will be substantiated and articulated.

➢ Sensitivity clusters will become easier to recognize.

➢ Sensitivity clusters highlight only areas in need of further investigation and not necessarily deception.

➢ When you locate several sensitivity clusters near each other, you can suspect deception but continue to investigate.

By following these guidelines, you can defend against CMD, and you'll discover what the liar doesn't want you to know. When you get that uneasy feeling about a questionable dialog or a written narrative, you will be able to make an intelligent decision as to believe it or not.

Now you're not going to take this into court, but you can't take the results of a polygraph examination into court either. Your analysis is not going to be something that you're going to rely on in a legal setting. I designed SHIELD Analysis to help you recognize signals of deception.

This process is going to tell you a lot about a speaker or writer. Take, for instance, you're listening to a politician, and they're explaining their platform or policies, but there's a volume of details they don't want you to know. You're going to use SHIELD Analysis to cut through all rhetoric and discover what's hidden in the language.

You'll find out what is real and what isn't. What are speakers or writers concealing in the language and what's the hidden intent? They can no longer hide their deception from you because now you have a tool to unmask them.

Now I know some of you feel this process is complicated, but I promise you I'm going to hold your hand and take you step-by-step through the process. You don't need a Ph.D. because even a grade-schooler can learn this.

When you begin this journey, remember that I am available to you anytime by email. If you have questions, reach out, and I'll help you where I can.

If you follow the rules, you learn the concepts, and before very long, you'll be an expert. You can work at home at your leisure, and the more you practice, the better you're going to get. You'll be surprised how much you pick up just from the information I provided you in this book.

If you decide to gain more training in the primary and intermediate course, you will be exposed to even more detail and explanations. But even if you go no further, you already have a skill lacking in nearly 95% of all Americans.

If you learn only one lesson from SHIELD Analysis, I guarantee you will be a better listener. You won't just hear a conversation; you will absorb it, process it, and automatically understand what the underlying details are.

There will be no further need for talking heads to explain what you just heard on the news. No one will have to explain the relevance to you. Whether you hear the truth or some media slanted version of their reality, you will immediately know for yourself if a lie is present.

Conclusion

My goal throughout this book was to expose you to what lying is all about and provide you with tools to defend against it. The average person doesn't usually have the skill or the high-powered software to screen information to determine its legitimacy.

While intuition is a great equalizer, it doesn't always provide enough insight to articulate a person's uneasiness when confronted with a potential lie. Consequently, one needs a tool he or she can rely on to provide some consistency and validation to internal feelings about potentially false information.

SHIELD Analysis is a language assessment technique designed to help you sort fact from fiction. Is it 100% accurate? It is not! But neither is your intuition or any other form of lie detection.

We try for the 100% level, and the more you practice with SHIELD Analysis, the better you will get. You will develop your assessment style, and I believe you'll be amazed at the deception you recognize even in the very beginning.

Once you familiarize yourself with the processes, you may wish to advance to higher levels of training. Eventually, you may even aspire to provide services to others as I have done for nearly fifteen years.

As you require more training, Western Legends Research is ready to offer intermediate and advanced levels. You experienced the Basic SHIELD Analysis Course in this book, along with a few extra tips.

The Intermediate SHIELD Analysis Course provides the next step in advancement. This intermediate course provides you with an opportunity to work through examples and exercises to practice what you learned. If you miss something, you can go back to this book or review the video for reinforcement of the concepts.

Eventually, maybe not so far in the future, you may wish to pursue the Advanced SHIELD Analysis Course. The advanced course is the full CMD diagnostics program where you will learn the uses and gain access to sophisticated software platforms like PCAD3, LIWC, TROPES, and LVA-4i.

These applications can provide you with answers in minutes rather than hours of in-depth analysis. At this point, you will have the skill to become a full-time practitioner or even an instructor. Can you envision yourself as the expert people come to with concerns before and after they have been the victims of deception?

Your new knowledge allows you to not only discover the deception, but you now have the skill to teach the techniques to others. These are the same techniques and software applications I use to reduce the time I spend in language and speech assessment.

Take your time with the learning process, and whether you learn by reading or by viewing videos, I'll teach you what you need to know. Honestly, this doesn't take a Ph.D. in some social science.

I have taught young people right out of high school as well as older adults well into their seventies.

The concepts are not complicated, and once you learn them, they will stay with you forever.

You will become more attentive to conversations and written communications. You'll learn to listen to people instead of just hearing them.

I hope you have enjoyed the book and found some benefit. I look forward to working with you to pursue higher levels of training. And as you advance, feel free to contact me anytime at:

WESTERN LEGENDS RESEARCH, LLC
P.O. Box 5343
Sun City West, AZ 85376-5343
Email: dtunnell@westernlegendsresearch.com
Web: https://www.westernlegendsresearch.com

Thank you for reading. Here's to your success in becoming an expert in the use of SHIELD Analysis and Psycholinguistics.

About the Author

DR. DALE TUNNELL was born in Powell, Wyoming, in 1951. He is a decorated Vietnam veteran, married and now living a retired lifestyle in Phoenix, Arizona.

Trained in psycholinguistics and psychological content analysis, Dale is a retired law enforcement officer with over forty years of service with federal, state, and local agencies. He earned his Master of Arts Degree in Management from Webster University and his Doctor of Philosophy Degree in Psychology from Capella University.

Dale received Beginning, Advanced, and Stage II training In Scientific Content Analysis at the Laboratory for Scientific Interrogation, in Phoenix, Arizona. He also mentored under Louis Gottschalk, MD, Ph.D., at the University of California at Irvine, where he acquired his expertise in Psychiatric Content Analysis and Diagnosis.

Dale served as a Senior Researcher for Nemesysco, Ltd, Netanya, Israel, and is recognized internationally as an expert in Layered Voice Analysis. He was also the Director of Forensic Intelligence and Research with Halcyon Group International.

He is an author of a previous book about the secrets William H. Bonney, alias Billy the Kid, nearly took with him to his grave. In his book, ***RESURRECTING THE DEAD,*** he used many of the methods described in this current book. Both books may be found on Amazon.com and numerous other booksellers, worldwide.

Dale is active member of the American Psychological Association and the Linguistic Society of America.

Dale L. Tunnell, Ph.D.

Made in the USA
Columbia, SC
03 February 2020